This copy of

The School Rules
Joke Book

belongs to

....

Other RED FOX joke books

THE SMELLY SOCKS JOKE BOOK By Susan Abbott
THE EVEN SMELLIER SOCKS JOKE BOOK by Karen King
BEST BROWNIE JOKES collected by Brownies
BEST CUB JOKES collected by Cub Scouts
SANTA'S CHRISTMAS JOKE BOOK by Katie Wales
THE BULLYBUSTERS JOKE BOOK by John Byrne
THE GOOD EGG YOLK BOOK by Katie Wales
THE MILLENNIUM JOKE BOOK by Sue Mongredien

SPLAT!

THE SCHOOL RULES JOKE BOOK

BY KAREN KING

Illustrated by
Andrew Warrington

RED FOX

A Red Fox Book

Published by Random House Children's Books
20 Vauxhall Bridge Road, London SW1V 2SA

A division of Random House UK Ltd
London Melbourne Sydney Auckland
Johannesburg and agencies throughout the world

1 3 5 7 9 10 8 6 4 2

Typeset by SX Composing DTP, Rayleigh, Essex
Printed and bound in Norway by AIT Trondheim AS

RANDOM HOUSE UK Limited Reg No. 954009

ISBN 0 09 940198 3

CONTENTS

TEACHERS' TALES

TEACHER: Can anyone tell me how many seconds there are in a year?
BRIGHT SPARK: Twelve, miss. January 2nd, February 2nd . . .

TEACHER: This is the third time I've told you off this week, Smithers. What have you got to say about that?
SMITHERS: Thank goodness it's Friday!

TEACHER: Sarah, didn't you hear me call you?
SARAH: Yes, but you told us not to answer back.

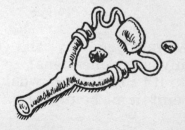

TEACHER: Kevin, why are you late for school again?

KEVIN: I stopped two boys fighting, sir.

TEACHER: Well done. How did you manage that?

KEVIN: I kicked both of them, sir.

TEACHER: Sadie, why are you crawling into school ten minutes late?

SADIE: Because you told me never to walk into school late again.

TEACHER: Risa, you missed school yesterday, didn't you?

RISA: No, sir, not a bit.

TEACHER: Ben, why can't you ever answer any of my questions?

BEN: If I could, there wouldn't be much point in me being here.

When the teacher entered the classroom, he noticed a little pool of water near the blackboard.

'Who is responsible for this?' he asked. No one replied.

'I want the person who did this to own up,' said the teacher. 'Everyone close your eyes, then the guilty person must come forward and write their name on the blackboard. No one must open their eyes until I say so.'

So everyone closed their eyes. Soon there were quiet footsteps over to the blackboard, a pause and then the sound of someone writing on it with chalk, followed by more footsteps.

When the teacher told everyone to open their eyes there was a loud gasp. Another little puddle of water had appeared next to the first, and on the blackboard was written, 'The Phantom Piddler Strikes Again!'

TEACHER: Now, children, this afternoon I'm going to tell you all about a gorilla. So pay attention, all of you. If you don't look at me you'll never know what a gorilla is.

TEACHER: What came after the Stone Age and the Bronze Age?
SUKI: The sausage!

TEACHER: Now, Sam, if I gave you three rabbits, then the next day I gave you five rabbits, how many would you have?
SAM: Nine, sir.
TEACHER: Nine?
SAM: Yes, sir. I've got one already!

ART TEACHER: Patsy, I told you all to draw a cow eating grass but you've only drawn the cow.
PATSY: That's 'cos the cow's eaten the grass, sir.

TEACHER: Now then, you're new here, aren't you? What's your name?
PUPIL: Albert Mickey Jones.
TEACHER: I see, well I'll call you Albert Jones then.
PUPIL: My dad won't like that.
TEACHER: Why not?
PUPIL: He doesn't like people taking the Mickey out of my name.

Why did the teacher wear dark glasses?
Because the class was so bright.

Did you hear about the cross-eyed
    teacher?
He couldn't control his pupils.

TEACHER: Why are you late, Mark?
MARK: Please, sir, the sign outside the
    school says, 'GO SLOW, CHILDREN!'

TEACHER: Why are you late, Kevin?
KEVIN: I must have over-washed, sir.

ATIF: I'm sorry I'm late, sir. I was having a dream about football.
TEACHER: How did that make you late for school?
ATIF: They played extra time.

TEACHER: Which family does the octopus belong to?
JENNY: No one in our street, sir.

SCIENCE TEACHER: James, give me the name of a liquid that won't freeze.
JAMES: Hot water, sir.

TEACHER: Does anyone know which month has twenty-eight days?
CLEVER CLIVE: All of them do, sir.

TEACHER: Smith, you're late again!
SMITH: Sorry, sir, I overslept.
TEACHER: You mean you sleep at home as well as here?

Why was the headmaster worried?
Because there were too many rulers in the school.

TEACHER (to noisy class): Every time I open my mouth, some fool speaks.

TEACHER: Jones, I told you to stand at the end of the line.
JONES: I know, sir, but there was already someone there.

TEACHER: If I bought a hundred currant buns for one pound, what would each bun be?
FREDDY: Stale, miss.

TEACHER: Kate, what is 'can't' short for?
KATE: Cannot, miss.
TEACHER: And what is 'don't' short for?
KATE: Doughnut, miss.

TEACHER: In 1940, what were the Poles doing in Russia?
HARRY: Holding up the telegraph wires.

TEACHER: Can anyone tell me what the Dog Star is?
SHEILA: Lassie, miss.

TEACHER: Why are you standing on your head?
PUPIL: I'm just turning things over in my mind, sir.

TEACHER: What's your name?
BOY: Henry.
TEACHER: Say 'sir'.
BOY: OK. Sir Henry.

The teacher told the class to write the longest sentence they could think of on the blackboard. One bright spark wrote, 'Imprisonment for life'!

TEACHER: Name four animals in the cat family.
JANE: Mummy cat, Daddy cat and two kittens.

Teacher, teacher, why do you call me
   'Pilgrim'?
Because you're making a little progress.

TEACHER: Which is the furthest away,
   America or the moon?
BETTY: America, miss. You can see the
   moon.

TEACHER: Johnny, find Australia on the
   map for me.
JOHNNY: There it is, sir.
TEACHER: Now, Susie, who discovered
   Australia?
SUSIE: Johnny did, sir.

SALLY: Please, sir, I wish we lived in the
   olden days.
TEACHER: Why's that?
SALLY: There wouldn't be so much history
   to learn.

TEACHER: Gillian, what kind of birds do we find in captivity?
GILLIAN: Jailbirds, sir.

TEACHER: What is the plural of mouse?
PUPIL: Mice.
TEACHER: Good. And what is the plural of baby?
PUPIL: Twins.

TEACHER: What is the longest word in the English language?
PUPIL: Smiles – because there's a mile between the first and last letters.

TEACHER: I despair of you, Ben. I don't see how it is possible to get so many things wrong in one day.
BEN: It's because I always get here early, sir.

TEACHER: Can anyone tell me what the wife of a sultan is called?

GARY: A sultana!

TEACHER: Amy, where are elephants found?

AMY: I dunno, miss. They're so big I didn't think they ever got lost!

TEACHER: If you add 53,917 to 47,891, divide the answer by three then multiply it by four, what do you get?

SID: The wrong answer, sir.

TEACHER: If there are five flies on this desk and I hit one with the ruler, how many will there be left?

SARAH: Just the squashed one, miss.

TEACHER: I wish you'd pay a little attention, Suzy.

SUZY: I'm paying as little as I can, miss.

TEACHER: In which part of the world are people the most ignorant?

JACK: London.

TEACHER: London! Why on earth do you say that?

JACK: The geography book says that's where the population is the most dense.

TEACHER: You seem to be very informed, Blake. Have you read Dickens?

BLAKE: No, sir.

TEACHER: Have you read Shakespeare?

BLAKE: No, sir.

TEACHER: Well, what have you read?

BLAKE: Er, I've got red hair, sir.

MUSIC TEACHER: Brian, if 'f' means *forte*, what does 'ff' mean?
BRIAN: Eighty.

TEACHER: Sam, 'R-O-X' doesn't spell rocks.
SAM: What does it spell then.

JANICE: Please, miss, do hams grow on plants?
TEACHER: No, of course they don't.
JANICE: Then what's an 'ambush', miss?

TEACHER: Today I'm going to instruct you on Mount Everest.
SAMMY: Will we be back for lunch, sir?

TEACHER: Fiona, give me a sentence containing the word 'gruesome'.
FIONA: My dad didn't shave for a week and grew some whiskers.

TEACHER: What is the climate of New Zealand like?

MATTHEW: Very cold, Sir.

TEACHER: Wrong.

MATTHEW: But, Sir, when they send us meat, it always arrives frozen.

HANNAH: What's the difference between wages and a salary, sir?

TEACHER: Well, if you get paid wages, you get paid every week, but if you get paid a salary, you get paid every month. For example, I get a salary and I'm paid every month.

HANNAH: Really? Where do you work, sir?

TEACHER: You're late! You should have been here at nine o'clock.

BILLY: Why, sir, what happened?

TEACHER: If eggs were fifty pence a dozen, how many would you get for thirty pence?

PUPIL: None.

TEACHER: None?

PUPIL: If I had thirty pence I'd buy a bag of crisps.

ANNE: What type of feet does a maths teacher have?
TIM: I don't know.
ANNE: Square feet.

TEACHER: Christopher, what is the opposite of misery?
CHRISTOPHER: Happiness, sir.
TEACHER: Good. And what is the opposite of sadness?
CHRISTOPHER: Gladness.
TEACHER: Excellent. And what is the opposite of woe?
CHRISTOPHER: Gee up.

TEACHER: Alan, give me a sentence starting with 'I'.
ALAN: I is—
TEACHER: No. You must always say 'I am . . .'
ALAN: OK. I am the ninth letter of the alphabet.

TEACHER: Jones, you're writing
has improved.
JONES: Thank you, sir.
TEACHER: Now I can see what
an awful speller you are.

TEACHER: What is an American Indian's
wife called?
DAVY: A squaw.
TEACHER: Correct. And what are
American Indian babies called?
DAVY: Squawkers.

TEACHER: Andy, I told you to write out
this poem twenty times because your
handwriting is so bad and you've only
written it out eleven times.
ANDY: Please, sir, my arithmetic is bad, too.

A teacher was talking to her class about the rewards of hard work. 'The ant is an example to us all,' she said. 'Every day the ant goes to work. Every day the ant is busy. And in the end what happens?'

A voice shouted from the back, 'Someone steps on it!'

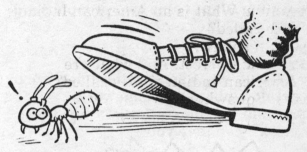

MOTHER: How was your first day at school, Timmy?

TIMMY: OK, except for some bloke called Sir, who kept spoiling the fun.

TEACHER: What can you tell me about the Dead Sea?

WINSTON: I didn't even know it was ill.

'Paul!' roared his father. 'Come here! What's all this about? Your teacher says he finds it impossible to teach you anything!'

'I told you he was no good,' said Paul.

MANDY: The craft teacher doesn't like
   what I'm making.
MOTHER: Why not? What are you
   making?
MANDY: Mistakes.

TEACHER: Alan, name two pronouns.
ALAN: Who? Me?

GARY: But, sir, I don't think I deserve to
   get nought for my homework.
TEACHER: You don't, but it's the lowest
   mark I can give you.

TEACHER: If I had four apples in my right
   hand and five apples in my left hand,
   what have I got?
CONRAD: Awfully big hands, sir.

Gary was leaning back in his chair, with
his feet stuck out in the aisle, chewing
gum noisily.
   'Gary!' shouted the teacher. 'Take that
chewing gum out of your mouth and put
your feet in this instant!'

TEACHER: David, how can you prove that the world is round?
DAVID: I didn't say it was, sir.

TEACHER: Why have you got cotton wool in your ears, Billy? Have you got an ear infection?
BILLY: No, sir. But you keep saying that everything you tell me goes in one ear and out of the other, so I'm trying to keep it in.

TEACHER: Darren, why weren't you in school yesterday?
DARREN: I was sick, sir.
TEACHER: Sick of what?
DARREN: Sick of school.

TEACHER: Who can tell me something of importance that didn't exist one hundred years ago?
TRACY: Me!

TEACHER: Who let the air out of the bus tyre?
DEREK: The nail did, sir!

TEACHER: What are you reading, Sam?
SAM: I dunno.
TEACHER: But you're reading aloud.
SAM: I know, but I'm not listening.

TEACHER: Goodness, David, what would you say if I came to school with a face like yours?
DAVID: I'd be too polite to mention it.

ROSIE: Miss, I ain't got a pencil.
TEACHER: No, Rosie, not *ain't*. I *haven't* got a pencil, they *haven't* got a pencil, we *haven't* got a pencil, you *haven't* got a pencil.
ROSIE: Gosh, miss, what's happened to all the pencils?

NUTTY KNOWLEDGE

Why does a flamingo lift up one leg?
If it lifted them both it would fall into the water.

Who invented fractions?
Henry the ⅛.

What does 'minimum' mean?
A very small mother.

What's the difference between a Spanish student and an English student?
Hundreds of miles.

What sleeps at the bottom of the sea?
A kipper.

What's the nearest thing to silver?
The Lone Ranger's bottom.

Why did Robin Hood only steal from the
   rich?
*Because the poor had nothing worth
   stealing.*

What kind of biscuit do you find at the
   South Pole?
A Penguin.

What is a
   skeleton?
*Bones with
   the person
   off.*

What is 'out
   of bounds'?
*An exhausted
   kangaroo.*

What is the most slippery country in the
   world?
Greece.

What do you eat in Paris?
The Trifle Tower.

If two's company and three's a crowd,
what are four and five?
Nine.

Who was the best actor in the Bible?
Samson. He brought the house down.

What kind of fish can't swim?
A dead one.

What do golfers use in China?
China tees.

What is the strongest bird in the world?
The crane.

What happens when you throw a green
stone in the Red Sea?
It gets wet.

What do people in Scotland eat?
Tart'n'pie.

What is a posthumous work?
*Something written by someone after
they're dead.*

Why is Russia a very fast place?
The people are always Russian (rushing).

What animal
has two
humps and
is found at
the North
Pole?
A lost camel.

Why is U.S. time behind
English time?
*Because England was discovered before
the United States.*

What do elves do after school?
Gnomework.

If athletes get athlete's foot,
what do astronauts get?
Missile toe.

What is a polygon?
A dead parrot.

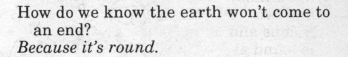

If Ireland fell into
the sea, which
county would float?
Cork.

How do we know the earth won't come to
an end?
Because it's round.

What do you get if you cross a U.S.
president with a shark?
Jaws Washington.

What's the quickest way to double your
money?
Fold it in half.

What is hail?
Hard-boiled rain.

What is Cheddar Gorge?
A large cheese sandwich.

What language do they speak in Cuba?
Cubic.

What is a myth?
A female moth.

What is an
    archaeologist?
*Someone whose career is
    in ruins.*

Which is the noisiest game?
*Tennis – because you can't play it without
    raising a racket.*

How many balls of string does it take to
    reach the moon?
One, if it's long enough.

Why do birds fly south in the winter?
Because it's too far to walk.

What holds the sun up in the sky?
Sunbeams.

What is a volcano?
A mountain with hiccups.

What is the fruitiest lesson?
History, because it's full of dates.

What is a prehistoric monster called when it's asleep?
A dinosnore.

How was the Roman Empire cut in half?
With a pair of Caesars.

How do Welsh people eat cheese?
Caerphilly.

Why doesn't the sea spill over the earth?
Because it's tide.

Who was the Black Prince?
Old King Cole's son.

What was King Arthur's court famous
   for?
Its knight life.

What has forty feet and sings?
The school choir.

Latin is a dead language,
It's as dead as dead can be.
It killed off all the Romans,
And now it's killing me!

Which kind of snakes can't do
   multiplication?
Adders.

Who was the world's greatest thief?
*Atlas, because he held up the whole
   world.*

Where do flies go in the winter?
*To the glassworks to be turned into
   bluebottles.*

Where do hamsters come from?
Hamsterdam.

Which is heavier, a full moon or
a half-moon?
*A half-moon because a full moon is
lighter.*

Which town in Britain makes terrible
sandwiches?
Oldham.

What do you call a robbery in Peking?
A Chinese takeaway.

Why do polar bears have fur coats?
Because they'd look silly in plastic macs.

Why are goldfish red?
The water makes them rusty.

Who invented fire?
Some bright spark.

Where does success come before work?
In the dictionary.

Why did stone-age man draw pictures of
  hippopotamuses and rhinoceroses on
  cave walls?
He couldn't spell their names.

Which animal is found on every legal
  document?
A seal.

Where do
  tadpoles
  change?
In a croakroom.

Why are
  astronauts
  successful
  people?
*Because they
  always go up
  in the world.*

Why is Alabama the smartest state in the U.S.?
It has four As and one B.

Which is the best hand to write with?
Neither. It's best to write with a pen.

What sort of animal is a slug?
A snail with a housing problem.

Who invented underground tunnels?
A mole.

What followed the dinosaur?
Its tail.

How do we know that Joan of Arc was French?
She was maid in France.

Which Elizabethan explorer could stop bikes?
Sir Francis Brake.

SILLY SPORTS

Two boys were having a boxing match
in the school hall. One of the boys was
swinging punches like fury but not
landing any. At the end of the round
he asked the games master how
he was doing.

'Not very well,' said the games master.
'But carry on with what you're doing – he
might catch a cold from the draughts!'

How do you service your pogo stick?
Give it a spring-clean.

Why were the members of the cricket
   team given lighters?
Because they kept losing their matches.

What's an insect's favourite game?
Cricket.

Did you hear about the two flies playing
football in a saucer?
They were practising for the cup.

If there's a referee in football and an
umpire in tennis, what do you have
in bowls?
Goldfish.

What does PT stand for?
Physical Torture.

CYRIL: Mum, can I have a new pair of
plimsolls for gym, please?
MUM: Why can't Jim buy his own?

Why did the boy come first in the 100 metre sprint?
He had athlete's foot.

Why couldn't the car play football?
Because it only had one boot.

PE TEACHER: Why didn't you stop that ball?
GOALIE: That's what the net's for, isn't it?

Knock, knock.
Who's there?
Penny.
Penny who?
Penalty pass against goal shooter.

Two boys were playing football. One boy tried a shot at goal, missed and said, 'I could kick myself.'

'Don't bother,' said his friend. 'You'll probably miss.'

Why did the games master put sawdust on the football pitch?
To stop the school team from slipping out of the league.

What ring is square?
A boxing ring.

FATHER: What position are you in the school football team, son?
SON: The games master says I'm the main drawback.

TEACHER (after football practice): Has anyone seen my glasses?
SAM: Yes, sir, you left them on the pitch.
TEACHER: Well, why didn't you give them to me?
SAM: I didn't think you'd want them after I stepped on them.

SUE: Why are tennis balls round?
MARY: Because if they were square, they wouldn't roll.

When is cricket a crime?
When there's a hit-and-run.

Why did the liquorice go jogging?
Because it was a liquorice-all-sport.

42

What's a Chinese golf teacher called?
Ho Lin Wun.

What do you call the man who teaches
 you PE?
Jim Nash.

What did the games teacher say to the
 girl who lost a hockey ball?
Find it quickly or I'll give you some stick.

What game goes round and round?
Rounders.

GAMES TEACHER: You never come first in
 anything.
KEVIN: I'm always first in the dinner
 queue.

GYM TEACHER: Why didn't you attempt
 the high jump, Watkins?
WATKINS: I'm scared of heights, sir.

What do you get when you cross a dive
 with a handstand?
A broken back.

What is the quietest game?
*Tenpin bowling, because you can hear a
pin drop.*

What has eleven heads and runs around
screaming?
A school hockey team.

What does the winner
lose in a race?
His breath.

Why is it funny to see a
boy run a mile?
*Because he really moves
two feet.*

Why did Cinderella get thrown out of the
rounders team?
*Because she kept running away from the
ball.*

GAMES TEACHER: Why didn't you do the
long jump, Smithers?
SMITHERS: Because I'm short-sighted, sir.

TEACHER: Why are you swimming on your back?
GWEN: Because I've just had lunch and it's dangerous to swim on a full stomach.

Susie came home from school looking really excited. 'Mum, I think I'm going to be in the school athletics team,' she said.
'That's good,' replied her mother. 'Why?'
'Because today the teacher said that if I carry on the way I'm going, I'll be for the high jump.'

Why is the football pitch always wet?
Because the players are always dribbling.

Can a match box?
No, but a tin can.

What's the difference between a nail and a bad boxer?
One is knocked in and the other is knocked out.

A schoolboy at the swimming baths climbed to the very top diving board. He lifted his arms and was just about to dive off when the teacher came running up, shouting, 'Don't dive – there's no water in the pool!'

'That's OK, sir,' said the boy. 'I can't swim!'

The PE teacher was telling the class how important it was to exercise regularly. 'Look at me, for example,' he said. 'I exercise every day and I can lift three hundred pounds.'

'That's nothing, sir,' shouted a boy at the back. 'I know a woman who can lift five hundred pounds.'

Good gracious, who's that?' gasped the teacher.

'A cashier at the bank, sir!'

MARK: Are you going to watch the school football match this afternoon?
CLIVE: No, it's a waste of time. I can tell you the score before the game starts.
MARK: Can you? What is it then?
CLIVE: Nil – nil.

The sports teacher was giving the class their very first cricket lesson.

'Now, who can tell me how to hold a bat?' he asked.

'By the wings, sir,' replied Andy.

Did you hear about the football team that was so bad the crowd changes were announced to the team?

Why did the American football coach go to the bank?
To get his quarter back.

If it takes a football team forty-five minutes to eat a ham, how long will it take three football teams to eat half a ham?
It depends on whether they're professional or am-eaters (amateurs).

TEACHER: Why are you late?
PAUL: Sorry, sir, I was practising my football.
TEACHER: Perhaps you ought to practise headball, it might affect your brain more than my lessons do!

VICKY: Our school team has got two
   Chinese footballers.
DAWN: Chinese footballers?
VICKY: Yes. We Won Once and How Long
   Since.

TEACHER: Now we're all going to play
   squash. Which side would you like to
   be on, Billy?
BILLY: The orange side, please.

There once was a large tabby cat,
Who swallowed a cricket bat.
He swallowed the ball,
The wickets and all,
So the cricket team clobbered him flat!

He drives us up the wall,
He puts us through the hoop,
We never have a ball,
To that he wouldn't stoop.
He really makes us crawl,
To him we bend our knee,
And with our arms outstretched,
We hail our teacher of PE.

DAFT DINNERS

There was an old man of Poole,
Who spent one day at school,
He ate a school dinner,
Which made him much thinner,
That poor old man of Poole.

Where is the best place to
    have the sickroom?
Next to the school canteen.

What do French pupils say when they've
    eaten their school
    dinners?
Mercy!

PUPIL: Cook, there
    are feathers in
    my custard.
COOK: I know, it's
    Bird's custard.

The pigs refuse to eat
Our leftovers of peas and meat.
Of course I don't blame,
I'd do the same,
And chuck it under the seat.

Why was the soup rich?
Because it had fourteen carrots in it.

What is a mushroom?
The school dining hall.

If you stay to school dinners,
Better throw them aside,
A lot of kids didn't,
A lot of kids died.

SAM: I've got two thousand bones in my
    body.
JIMMY: How come?
SAM: I had fish for dinner at school.

Why does the school cook dip sponge
    fingers in paraffin?
To make them light, of course.

PUPIL: Cook, this chicken has spots on it.
COOK: That's OK, it's only chickenpox.

What's yellow, thick and often found on schoolboys' ties?
School custard.

Did you hear about the cruel school cook?
She beats the eggs and whips the cream.

What's the difference between school tapioca and frogspawn?
Not a lot.

MUM: Billy, from now on you're going to have free school dinners.
BILLY: But, Mum, I don't want three school dinners – it's bad enough eating one!

We had cottage pie yesterday. The council came round and condemned it.

The meat is made of iron,
The spuds are made of steel,
And if those don't get you,
The afters surely will.

FREDDY: What's that fly doing on your school dinner?
SID: It probably died after tasting it.

The dinners at our school are so cold that even the potatoes wear their jackets.

How did the dinner lady get an electric shock?
She stepped on a bun and a currant went up her leg.

TEACHER: Mark, why are you the only
child in the classroom today?
MARK: 'Cos I'm the only one who didn't
have a school dinner yesterday.

What's worse than finding a caterpillar
in your school salad?
Finding half a caterpillar.

Can school peas get married?
Not if they're Bachelor's.

MARY: This egg is bad.
DINNER LADY: Well don't blame me. I only
laid the table.

STEVE: I think my mum wants me to leave home. She always wraps my lunch in a road map.

DINNER LADY: Now eat up your greens, there's a good girl. They're very good for your skin, you know.
SUSIE: But I don't want green skin!

Our school dinners are so bad, pygmies come from Africa to dip their arrows in them.

A schoolboy dining in Crewe,
Found quite a large mouse in his stew.
The cook said, 'Don't shout,
And wave it about,
Or the others will all want one too!'

PUPIL: I thought you said there was a choice for dinner, but there's only sausage and mash.
DINNER LADY: That's the choice, take it or leave it.

School dinners are very tasty – I had one last week and I can still taste it.

TEACHER: This coffee tastes like mud.
OTHER TEACHER: It was only ground this
morning.

SALLY: What's the best day to fry eggs?
JOHN: Fry-day.

JEFF: What cake wanted to rule the
world.
KATE: Attila the Bun.

There was a young boy from Crewe,
A Cheshire lad, through and through.
He ate a school dinner,
And he was the winner,
Of the race to get to the loo!

DINNER LADY: Jemima, it's
very rude to reach
over the table for
cakes. Haven't you
got a tongue in your
head?
JEMIMA: Yes, miss,
but my arms are
longer.

PUPIL: Sir, are caterpillars good to eat?
TEACHER: Of course not. Why do you ask?
PUPIL: 'Cos you've just eaten one on your
  lettuce.

NEW TEACHER: Ugh! This coffee tastes
  like soap.
OTHER TEACHER: That must be tea – the
  coffee tastes like glue.

TOM: Cook, there's a worm on my plate!
COOK: That isn't a worm, it's your
  sausage.

NICK: Cook, I can't eat this!
COOK: Why not?
NICK: I haven't got a knife and fork.

Knock, knock.
Who's there?
Cook.
Cook who?
That's the first one I've heard this year.

How do you start a pudding race?
Sa-go.

When are school dinners noisy?
When they are bangers and mash.

LITTLE BOY: Cook, I don't like cheese with holes!

COOK: Eat the cheese then and leave the holes on the side of your plate.

Knock, knock.
Who's there?
Alick.
Alick who?
Alick my lollipop.

Knock, knock.
Who's there?
Jaws.
Jaws who?
Jaws one Cornetto.

LEROY: There's a button in my soup.

DINNER LADY: It must have fallen off when the salad was dressing.

KAVITA: What's green and goes boing-boing-boing?

CHLOE: A spring cabbage!

Knock, knock.
Who's there?
Bernadette.
Bernadette who?
Bernadette all my dinner and now I'm
*   starving!*

There was a fat teacher called Bet,
Who sat in the classroom and ate.
She spent all her cash,
On bangers and mash,
And ended up with a ninety pounds debt.

There was a young schoolboy from
Surrey,
Who cooked up a large pot of curry.
He ate the whole lot,
Straight from the pot,
Then ran to the tap in a hurry.

Why did the schoolboy
    keep a mince pie in
    his comic?
He liked crummy jokes.

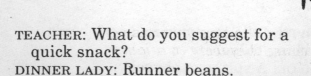

TEACHER: What do you suggest for a
    quick snack?
DINNER LADY: Runner beans.

There was a young teacher from Dewy,
Who couldn't eat meat that was chewy,
Nor the milk, nor the fish,
That was put on his dish,
He'd only eat piles of chop suey.

STEVE: What's round, white and giggles?
GOPAL: A tickled onion.

There was a schoolboy called Freddie,
Who ate several helpings of jelly,
Then rhubarb and custard,
And sausage and mustard,
Which gave him a pain in the belly.

Knock, knock.
Who's there?
Dana.
Dana who?
Dana talk with your mouth full.

What kind of biscuit flies?
A plain biscuit.

Why did the strawberries cry?
Because they were in a jam.

Knock, knock.
Who's there?
General Lee,
General Lee who?
General Lee I hate school dinners.

Knock, knock.
Who's there?
Howell.
Howell who?
*Howell you have your toast, with
    marmalade or jam?*

What do you do with a blue banana?
Try to cheer it up.

Knock, knock.
Who's there?
Pudding.
Pudding who?
*Pudding on your
shoes before your
trousers is a bad idea.*

Did you hear about the farmer who ploughed his field with a steamroller because he wanted to grow mashed potatoes?

SOO: What's served in glasses and is difficult to swallow?
CHAI: A stiff drink!

Why did the apple turnover?
Because it saw the jam roll.

JASON: My plate's wet!
DINNER LADY: Don't be silly, that's the soup!

What sits in custard looking cross?
Apple grumble.

Knock, knock.
Who's there?
Four eggs.
Four eggs who?
Four eggs ample.

There was a young teacher from Ryde,
Who ate some green apples and died.
The apples fermented,
Inside the lamented,
And made cider inside her inside.

There once was a schoolboy called Kidd,
Who ate twenty pies for a quid.
When they asked, 'Are you faint?'
He replied, 'No, I ain't,
But I don't feel as well as I did.'

Little Jack Horner,
Sat in the corner,
Eating his cold meat pie.
He caught salmonella,
The unfortunate fella,
And now he's likely to die.

EXASPERATING EXAMS

Roses are red,
Violets are blue,
I copied your exam paper,
And I failed too.

EXAMINER: Never mind what the date is, Alan, get on with the exam.
ALAN: But, sir, I want to get something right.

TEACHER: Why do you always fail your exams?
PUPIL: Because I always get the wrong exam paper.

EXAM QUESTION: Where are the Andes?
PUPIL'S ANSWER: On the end of my armes.

EXAMINER: Mark, I told you not to look in your bag. You could have the answers.

MARK: I'm not, sir. I'm looking in Paul's bag – he's got the answers.

Knock, knock.
Who's there?
Exam.
Exam who?
Eggs, ham and cheese.

FATHER: How did you get on with your maths test today?

SON: I only got one sum wrong.

FATHER: Well done. How many sums were there?

SON: Twelve.

FATHER: So you got eleven right?

SON: No – they were the ones I couldn't do.

EXAM QUESTION: Where is Felixstowe?

PUPIL'S ANSWER: On the end of Felix's foot.

EXAM QUESTION: In Great Britain, where are kings and queens usually crowned?

PUPIL'S ANSWER: On the head.

EXAM QUESTION: What did James I do on coming to the throne?
PUPIL'S ANSWER: He sat on it.

EXAM QUESTION: What are the chief minerals to be found in Cornwall?
PUPIL'S ANSWER: Coca-Cola and orangeade.

FATHER: How did your exams go, Tommy?
TOMMY: Great, Dad. I nearly got ten in every subject.
FATHER: What do you mean – nearly ten?
TOMMY: Well, I got the nought.

Tommy was saying his prayers. 'God bless my mum and dad and please make Montreal the capital of Canada.'

'Why did you say that, Tommy?' asked his mother.

'Because that's what I wrote in my exam,' explained Tommy.

Knock, knock.
Who's there?
Sammy.
Sammy who?
Sammyxams we got to do?

DAD: Well, Billy, did you pass your exams?
BILLY: No, Dad, but I came top of those that failed.

EXAM QUESTION: Why was the period between 500 AD and 4200 AD known as the Dark Ages?
PUPIL'S ANSWER: Because those were the days of the knights.

After an exam the teacher said to a boy, 'Why have you written by some of your questions, "See Simon Taylor's paper"?' The boy replied, 'Well, sir, you said we weren't to copy each other's work.'

EXAM QUESTION: What was the Romans' greatest feat?
PUPIL'S ANSWER: Learning Latin.

EXAMINER: You will be allowed half an hour for each question.
PUPIL: How long can we have for the answer, sir?

MOTHER: Your history exam marks aren't very good, Samantha.

SAMANTHA: It isn't my fault. My teacher keeps asking me questions about things that happened before I was born.

FATHER: Well, David, did you get a good place in the exams?

DAVID: Yes, Dad, right by the radiator.

FATHER: Why are your exam marks so low?

SON: Because I sit at the desk at the back, Dad.

FATHER: What difference does that make?

SON: Well, there are so many of us in the class that when it's my turn for marks there aren't any left.

Exams, exams,
I wonder what they're for?
Exams are made to teach us,
But they're a terrible bore.

What exams does Santa Claus take?
Ho, ho, ho levels.

Why is an optician like an examiner?
They both test pupils.

MUSIC EXAMINER: Is there anything
    special you'd like to play?
MANDY: Yes, miss, truant!

The exam question was to write an essay
on water. One child wrote, 'Water is a
colourless liquid that turns dark when
you wash in it.'

EXAMINER: Smith, you've copied Brown's
    exam paper, haven't you?
SMITH: How did you find out, sir?
EXAMINER: His paper says, 'I don't know'
    and yours says, 'neither do I'.

FATHER: How are your
    exam marks,
    son?
SON: They're
    under
    water.
FATHER: What
    do you mean?
SON: Below C level.

TEE HEE!

EXAMINER: Christopher, can you explain to me how you've got exactly the same answers as David in the maths test?

CHRISTOPHER: We used the same pencil, sir.

FATHER: This report is terrible, Martin. It says that in your exams you came bottom in a class of twenty.

MARTIN: It could be worse, Dad, there could be more people in the class.

During an exam the teacher saw one of the boys peering over at another boy's paper. So she went over to the boy's desk and said, 'Kevin, I hope I didn't see you looking at that boy's paper.' To which Kevin replied, 'I hope you didn't either, miss.'

What's black and white and extremely difficult?
An exam paper.

EXAM QUESTION: Who were the Peelers?

PUPIL'S ANSWER: The followers of William of Orange.

MOTHER: Why are your exam marks so poor this term, Anna?

ANNA: It's the teacher's fault, Mum.

MOTHER: But you had the same teacher last term and you did well in your exams then.

ANNA: Yes, but I'm not sitting by the brainiest girl in the class now. The teacher's moved her.

MABEL: What's your Eric going to be when he's passed his exams?

ETHEL: The way he's going, a pensioner, I should think!

What exams do farmers take?
Hay levels.

Who got the best marks in the animal exam?
The cheetah.

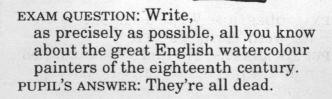

EXAM QUESTION: Write, as precisely as possible, all you know about the great English watercolour painters of the eighteenth century.

PUPIL'S ANSWER: They're all dead.

EXAM QUESTION: When was Napoleon born?
PUPIL'S ANSWER: On his birthday.

EXAM QUESTION: What's the difference between unlawful and illegal?
PUPIL'S ANSWER: Unlawful is against the law, and illegal is a sick bird.

MUM: How did your music exam go?
BRIAN: The music teacher said my playing was out of this world.
MUM: Really?
BRIAN: Well – she said it was unearthly.

EXAM QUESTION: Write a sentence with the word 'fascinate' in it.
PUPIL'S ANSWER: My Dad's waistcoat has nine buttons but he can only fasten eight.

EXAM QUESTION: What's a Grecian urn?
PUPIL'S ANSWER: About twenty pounds a
  week.

EXAM QUESTION: What happens to gold
  when it is exposed to air?
PUPIL'S ANSWER: It's stolen.

EXAM QUESTION: Who were the
  Phoenicians?
PUPIL'S ANSWER: The people who
  invented Phoenician blinds.

EXAMINER: Did you make
  this poem up
  yourself,
  Donna?
DONNA: Yes,
  sir, every
  word.
EXAMINER:
  Well,
  pleased to
  meet you,
  William
  Shakespeare!

GRAFFITI
GAGS

Our school is a good
   school,
It's made of bricks and
   plaster,
The only thing that's wrong
   with it,
Is the bald headmaster.

He laughed when they said it couldn't be
   done,
He smiled and said he knew it,
But he tried the thing that couldn't be
   done,
And found he couldn't do it.

Don't go to school – sleep at home.

Poor old teacher, we missed you so,
When in hospital you had to go.
For you to remain there is a sin,
We're sorry about the banana skin.

Cut education costs – play truant.

May your life be like toilet paper – long and useful.

There's nothing wrong with this school that an atomic bomb wouldn't put right.

There was a young caretaker named
   Frank,
Who kept all his beer in the school tank.
One day it was locked,
And he was so shocked,
Because without his pint he'd go blank.

Our school is so posh we don't do vulgar fractions.

Education is a wonderful thing – it's wasted on children.

When things get twisted and out of joint,
Don't get discouraged and quit the game,
Remember a corkscrew never goes
   straight to the point,
But it gets there just the same.

Keep smiling – it makes everyone wonder
what you're up to.

The joke you just told isn't funny one bit,
It's pointless and dull, wholly lacking in
    wit.
It's so old and so stale it's beginning to
    smell –
And besides, it's the one *I* was going to
    tell.

I used to be conceited
but now I'm perfect.

We all sprang from monkeys but
some didn't spring far enough.

Those who can, do; those who can't teach!
I am a nut
I am a clown
That's why you read this
Upside down.

This school is so posh it's an approved school.

Why did the little girl take a hammer to school?
It was breaking-up day.

Mary had a little
    bear,
To which she was
so kind,
And everywhere
    that Mary
went,
She had a bear
    behind.

Never drink water – if it can rust iron, imagine what it can do to your stomach.

Don't worry if your job is small,
And your rewards are few.
Remember that the mighty oak,
Was once a nut like you.

Go to school to learn the three Rs:
Ravage, Riot and Revolution.

Where is the school
    spirit?
*He only haunts at
    night.*

There was a young
teacher of Rheims,
Who had the most frightening dreams.
She would wake in the night,
In a terrible fright,
Shaking the house with her screams.

I wish I was a little grub,
With whiskers round my tummy.
I'd climb into a honey pot
And make my tummy gummy.

Keep the school tidy – throw your
rubbish out of the windows.

Jack and Jill went up the hill,
To fetch a pail of water.
Jack fell down and broke his crown,
And Jill said, 'You twit! Now I'll have to
    fill the bucket up again!'

It's a dog's delight,
To bark and bite,
And little birds to sing.
And if you sit,
On a red-hot brick,
It's the sign of an early spring.

Humpty Dumpty sat on the wall,
Humpty Dumpty had a great fall.
All the king's horses,
And all the king's men,
Said, 'Scrambled eggs for dinner again!'

There was a headmaster from Quebec,
Who wrapped both his legs round his
    neck,
But then he forgot,
How to untie the knot,
And now he's an absolute wreck.

Our teacher's a peach – she's
got a heart of stone!

If you notice this notice you may have noticed that this notice is not Worth noticing!!!

There was a teacher from Niger,
Who went for a ride on a tiger.
Not long after that,
The tiger got fat,
With the lady from Niger inside her.

There was a young teacher from Harrow,
Whose nose was too long and too narrow,
It gave so much trouble,
That he bent it up double,
And wheeled it around school in a
barrow.

There was an old teacher called Leach,
Who took the whole class to the beach.
It said on a sign,
'Watch out for the mine—'
The last thing they heard
was his screech.

79

There was a teacher called McGees,
Who thought he was going to sneeze.
The class said, 'Atchoo!'
McGees caught the flu,
And blew the class into the trees!

There once was a teacher from Leeds,
Who swallowed a packet of seeds.
In less than an hour,
Her nose was a flower,
And her hair was a bunch of weeds.

A wonderful bird is the pelican,
His beak holds more,
Than his belly can.

I eat peas with honey,
I've done it all my life,
It makes the peas taste funny,
But it keeps them on the knife.

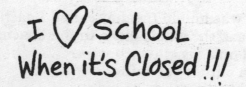

I ♡ School
When it's Closed !!!

Will the person who took my ladder
please return it, or further steps will be
taken.
   Signed,
   the Caretaker.

There was a young teacher called Emma,
Who was seized with a terrible tremor.
She swallowed a spider,
Which wriggled inside her,
And left Emma in an awful dilemma.

Our teacher's a treasure – we wonder
where she was dug up!

There was an old
   teacher called Green,
Who invented a caning
machine.
On the ninety-ninth stroke,
The rotten thing broke,
And hit poor Green on the beam!

Our geography teacher is so bad he got
lost showing some parents around the
school.

I like teachers – when they're at home!

Don't be late for school in the morning –
stay in bed until the afternoon.

Kick, kick.
Who's there?
Teacher.
Teacher who?
*Teach yer to fix
     the knocker.*

There was a young teacher called Fisher,
Who was fishing for fish in a fissure.
When a seal, with a grin,
Pulled the teacher right in,
And now they're fishing the fissure for
     Fisher.

A teacher who looks like a bear,
Fell soundly asleep in his chair.
He woke with loud screaming,
Because he was dreaming,
His pupils had shaved off his hair.
Our school bus crashed 'cos the driver
was upstairs collecting the fares.

Teacher is an anagram of cheater.

There was a headmaster in Spain,
Who misguidedly prayed for rain.
The resultant showers,
Lasted for hours,
And washed his school down the drain.

My teacher used to be a werewolf, but
she's howl right now.

A head by the name of Wally,
Had a girlfriend called Pretty Polly.
But he'd never kiss,
The pretty young miss,
'Cos Wally preferred a lolly.

The rain in Spain falls mainly on the
plain, but over here it always falls in the
school holidays!

There was a teacher called Mohammed
    Ben Tonki,
Who went for a walk on a donkey.
Then it suddenly spoke,
This miraculous moke,
And said 'Get off and walk, I feel wonky!'

I'm teacher's pet – she can't afford a dog.

Hickory, Dickory, Dock,
Two mice ran up the clock.
The clock struck one,
But the other one escaped with only
    minor injuries.

What do you get when you cross a
    professor with a monster?
A teacher from the Black Lagoon.

Teachers are very special – they're in a
class of their own.

There's a peanut sitting on the railway
    track,
His heart is all aflutter,
The train comes roaring round the bend,
Toot! Toot! – Peanut butter!

What's the difference between a teacher
and a train?
*One goes, 'Spit out your gum!' and the
   other goes, 'Choo! Choo!'*

Teacher on the railway, picking up stones,
Along came a train and broke Teacher's
   bones.
'Hey,' said Teacher. 'That's not fair!'
            'Tough!' said the
                 driver. 'I don't
                 care!'

                 A rabbit raced a
                 tortoise,
             You know the
         tortoise won,
     And Mr Rabbit came in late,
A little hot cross bun!

My teacher has turned into a bat.
He keeps hanging around me.

During dinner at the Ritz,
My teacher had forty fits.
And what made my sorrow greater
still, I was left to pay the bill!

When our headmaster retired we gave
  him an illuminating address.
We set fire to his house!

A bird in the hand can make a terrible
  mess.

PLAYGROUND PUNS

I like going to school; I like going home;
it's the bit in between I don't like.

I think my teacher is a card player – he
shuffles as he walks.

MANDY: I wish we could sell our teachers.
BEN: Why?
MANDY: 'Cos I read that at auctions Old
  Masters are fetching big prices.

SCHOOL BULLY: Are you trying to make a fool out of me?

CHEEKY CLIVE: No, I never interfere with nature.

TEACHER: Who gave you that black eye, Simon?

SIMON: No one gave it to me, sir. I had to fight for it.

Sid was the school swot. The other children used to pick him up and swot flies with him.

GIRL: What nationality are you?

FRIEND: Well, my mother was born in Iceland and my father was born in Cuba so I guess that makes me an ice cube.

Did you hear about the schoolboy who turned up at school with only one glove on? The teacher asked him why and he replied, 'Well, the weather forecast said that it might be warm, but on the other hand it might be quite cool'.

GARY: What did you get for Christmas?

MARK: A mouth organ. It's the best present I've ever had.

GARY: Why?

MARK: My mum gives me one pound a week not to play it.

Two boys were fighting in the playground. The teacher separated them and said sternly, 'You mustn't behave like that! You must learn to give and take.'

'We did, miss,' replied one of the boys. 'He took my crisps and I gave him a thump.'

Why did the headmaster move the
chickens out of the playground?
*So the pupils wouldn't overhear foul
language.*

BOY: Can you fight?
OTHER BOY: No.
BOY: Put 'em up you coward!

Weeee

What's a cheerful
flea called?
A hoptimist.

Knock, knock.
Who's there?
Gladys.
Gladys who?
Gladys Friday.

TEACHER: You've been fighting again, William, and this time you've lost both your front teeth.

WILLIAM: No, I haven't, miss. They're in my coat pocket.

BOY: I'm a born leader – I'm always the first out of school.

JIMMY: Mum, I've been banned from science lessons.

MOTHER: Why's that?

JOHNNY: Because I blew something up.

MOTHER: What?

JOHNNY: School!

Little Billy stamped in the house, threw his schoolbag on a chair and announced, 'I'm not going there again!'

'Whatever's the matter?' asked his mother.

'I can't read, I can't write and they won't let me talk, so what's the use?' demanded Billy.

SUE: My best friend isn't coming back to school, she's gone to the Caribbean.

ALICIA: Jamaica?

SUE: No, she went of her own accord.

CHRIS: What did the teacher say when he saw a herd of elephants coming over the hill wearing sunglasses?

DEREK: Nothing. He didn't recognise them.

MOTHER: Why don't you like your new teacher?

MAY: Because she told me to come and sit at the front for the present, and she never gave me a present.

KATY: Mum, I've been banned from cookery lessons because I burnt something.

MOTHER: Well that doesn't sound too terrible. What did you burn?

KATY: The school kitchen.

What happened when Moses had a
  headache?
God gave him some tablets.

SUNITA: What's the formula for water?
RUTH: H-I-J-K-L-M-N-O.
SUNITA: What?
RUTH: Teacher said it was H to O.

SALLY: Which word of five letters has six
  left when you take two away?
JANET: I don't know.
SALLY: Sixty

BOY: Why is a banana skin on a
  pavement like music?
FRIEND: I don't know.
BOY: Because if you don't C sharp you'll
  B flat.

GARY: Did you hear about the scientist
  who crossed a parrot with an alligator?
JOHN: No, what happened?
GARY: It bit his leg off and said, 'Who's a
  pretty boy, then?'

RACHEL: Did you hear about the bowl of daffodils in the maths classroom?
ALAN: No, what happened?
RACHEL: They grew square roots.

What do you call a jacket that's on fire?
A blazer.

RICARDO: Why don't elephants ride bicycles?
ANNA: They haven't got thumbs to ring the bell with.

Knock, knock.
Who's there?
Wendy.
Wendy who?
Wendy red, red, robin comes bob, bob, bobbin' along.

Why did the schoolboy take a ladder to
    school?
It was high school.

What do you call a frozen
    bike?
An icicle.

Why are tall people lazy?
Because they lie longer in bed.

What runs but can't walk?
Water.

I'd give my right arm to be ambidextrous.

Knock, knock.
Who's there?
Sadie.
Sadie who?
Sadie ten times table twice.

What's battery-powered and good for
    dead fish?
A herring aid.

CARETAKER: Who broke the window?
CARLOS: It was Ben, sir. He ducked when
I threw a stone at him.

Knock, knock.
Who's there?
Olive.
Olive who?
Olive just around the corner.

There was a schoolboy called Sid,
A totally stupid kid.
He gave his best hat,
To a greedy cat,
Now Sid wears a dustbin lid.

What makes grass so dangerous?
The blades.

LEROY: What is grey and hairy?
GARY: A school jumper.

Knock, knock.
Who's there?
Sis.
Sis who?
Sis any way to treat a friend?

What's got two legs, two arms and is
good on a dark night?
A light-headed man.

JANE: What did the flea say to the other
flea?
BARRY: Shall we walk or take the cat?

Why do elephants have trunks?
*Because they'd look pretty stupid with
suitcases.*

Did you hear about the schoolboy who
   put on a clean pair of socks every day?
*By the end of the week he couldn't get his
   shoes on.*

What makes an octopus a good fighter?
He's very well-armed.

Why did the chicken cross the road?
For fowl purposes.

MATTHEW: Why did the pretty
   schoolteacher marry the caretaker?
SINEAD: He swept her off her feet.

Knock, knock.
Who's there?
Sinbad.
Sinbad who?
Sinbad and you'll never go to heaven.

GRANT: What's wrapped in Clingfilm and
   lives in bell towers?
PETER: The Lunchpack of Notre Dame.

What's bright blue and weighs four
   tonnes?
An elephant holding its breath.

ALBERTO: What do you get if you cross a
   vicar with your school uniform?
MONICA: Holy clothes.

TAMMIE: What did the school tie say to
   the beret?
LUKE: You go on a head while I hang
   around.

Why did the caretaker give up his job?
Because he found that grime doesn't pay.

GWEN: What did one
wall say to the other
wall?
SALLY: I'll meet you at
the corner.

Why was the fly
dancing on the top
of the Coke bottle?
*Because it said 'Twist
to open'.*

CLAIRE: Who's bigger,
Mr Bigger or baby
Bigger?
RAMONA: Baby Bigger 'cos he's a little
bigger.

What should you do if your dog swallows
your dictionary?
Take the words right out of his mouth?

GARY: What time was it when Sir Lancelot looked at his bellybutton?
MARK: The middle of the knight.

SUKI: What can a bottle of soda hold that a million men can't?
TANYA: A bubble.

BOBBY: What sort of car has your dad got?
TOM: I can't remember the name. I think it starts with T.
BOBBY: Really? Ours only starts with petrol.

SCHOOL BULLY: What do you mean by telling everyone I'm an idiot?
TIMID TONY: Sorry. I didn't know it was meant to be a secret.

ANDREW: My dad's an explorer.
TESSA: Is he?
ANDREW: Yes, he works for British Rail.

CAREERS OFFICER: And have you a career in mind, Martin?

MARTIN: Well, I think I'd make a good book-keeper.

CAREERS OFFICER: Why's that?

MARTIN: I've sometimes kept library books for years and years.

Knock, knock.
Who's there?
Juno.
Juno who?
Juno what time it is?

STACEY: Who never minds being interrupted in the middle of a sentence?

TINA: A convict.

HARRY: I don't think my woodwork teacher likes me.

STUART: Why not?

HARRY: He's teaching me how to make a coffin.

JENNY: I haven't slept for days.

SARA: Why not?

JENNY: I usually sleep at night.

Anna was practising her singing lessons at home. Her younger brother sighed and said, 'I wish you'd practise singing Christmas carols.'

'Why?' asked Anna.

'Then you'd only have to sing once a year.'

One day, little Davey limped into the school playground with a bandage wrapped around his foot.

'Goodness, what have you done to your foot?' asked the teacher on duty.

'Tim fell on it,' said Davey.

'Tim who?'

'Tim-ber!'

What goes right up to school but never goes in it?
The path.

What's everyone's favourite saying at school?
I don't know.

OUTRAGEOUS OUTINGS

A class went on a school trip to Rome. On the Sunday they all went to church and when they came out the teacher said, 'I hope you all behaved.'

'Oh, yes, sir,' said one girl. 'A kind man offered me a plate full of money but I said, "no thanks".'

BOB: Our school cruise was a great success but a lot of kids had to be turned away.
CHRIS: Why?
BOB: The raft only held fifteen people.

There was a teacher from China,
Who took a trip on an ocean liner.
She slipped on the deck,
And twisted her neck,
Now she can see what's going on behind
her.

Tommy had been on a camping trip for a
few days.

'Did your tent leak?' asked his dad
when he returned.

'Only when it rained,' said Tommy.

What is a Laplander?
A clumsy girl on a school trip.

A party of schoolchildren from the city went on a trip to the country. One of them found a pile of empty milk bottles and shouted, 'Look, miss, I've found a cow's nest!'

Where's the worst trip you're likely to go on?
To the headmaster's office.

Anna had been on a school trip today.
'Our school bus had a puncture,' she told her mum when she returned.
'Oh dear, how did that happen?' asked her mum.
'There was a fork in the road,' Anna told her.

Brenda came home from school looking a bit worried. 'Today our teacher said, "We shall fight on the beaches, we shall fight on the airfields, we shall fight on the streets".'
'Ah, yes,' said her father. 'Those are the words of Winston Churchill.'
'Oh,' said Brenda, looking relieved. 'I thought he was talking about our school trip to France.'

A teacher took her class on a nature trail through the woods. She stopped by a tree and said, 'Brian, can you tell me what the outer part of a tree is called?'

'I don't know, sir,' said Brian.

'Bark, boy, bark!' said the teacher.

'OK, sir,' said Brian. 'Woof! Woof!'

WOOF WOOF!

BRIAN: Am I going on the school trip, sir?
TEACHER: Yes, if you don't behave yourself.

DAD: Did you enjoy your school trip?
ANNIE: Yes. We're going again tomorrow.
DAD: Why?
ANNIE: Search party.

THE SCHOOL OUTING

TEACHER: Well, class, this year's outing will be to the seaside.

CLASS: Hooray!

TEACHER: It will cost fifty pounds—

CLASS: Boo!

TEACHER: —by train, or two pounds by coach.

CLASS: Hooray!

TEACHER: The headmaster will be coming—

CLASS: Boo!

TEACHER: —to see us off.

CLASS: Hooray!

TEACHER: The weather will be wet and windy—

CLASS: Boo!

TEACHER: —in China and warm and sunny in England.

CLASS: Hooray!

TEACHER: There will be no paddling—

CLASS: Boo!

TEACHER: —until we get there.

CLASS: Hooray!

TEACHER: Lunch will be boiled fish and cabbage—

CLASS: Boo!

TEACHER: —for me and crisps, Coke and chocolate for you.

CLASS: Hooray!

TEACHER: There will be a visit to the
  museum—
CLASS: Boo!
TEACHER: —or, if preferred, to the
  funfair.
CLASS: Hooray!
TEACHER: But we must be back by twelve
  o'clock—
CLASS: Boo!
TEACHER: —midnight!
CLASS: Hooray!

Now, children,' said the teacher as the
  school party was about to board the
  Channel ferry. 'What do we say if one
  of the pupils falls into the sea?'
Up went Sam's hand. 'Pupil overboard,
sir!'
'Very good,' said the teacher. 'And what
do we say if one of the teachers falls into
the sea?'
'It depends which teacher it is, sir.'

Angela was telling her aunt about her school trip to Switzerland. Her aunt had never been to there. 'What's the scenery like?' she asked.

'Oh, I couldn't see much because of all the mountains,' replied Angela.

DAD: How did you enjoy your school trip to the seaside, son?
DEREK: OK, Dad, but a crab bit my toe.
DAD: Which one?
DEREK: Dunno. All crabs look alike to me.

GRAN: Did you go on your school trip today?
KATE: Yes, Gran.
GRAN: Which was the best bit?
KATE: Going home.

The school teacher and his class finally
arrived at the airport after a long,
fraught coach trip, ready to catch their
flight to Switzerland for the skiing
holiday.

'Oh dear, I wish I'd brought my piano,'
sighed Jimmy.

'Whatever for?' asked his teacher.

'I left my plane ticket on it!' Jimmy
told him.

Why did one school trip take longer than
the other, yet they were going to the
same place and started out at the same
time?
*One coach was going faster than the other
one.*

ALEX: Mum, I need a ladder for school.
MUM: Why?
ALEX: Our teacher said we were going on
a climbing holiday.

On a trip to the art gallery, a teacher
was annoyed to see a boy slapping a
statue. He marched over and demanded,
'Why are you slapping that statue?'

'Because the gallery attendant told me
to beat it,' replied the boy.

A young teacher wanted to introduce her class to the delights of classical music, so she arranged an outing to an afternoon concert at the Royal Albert Hall. To make the occasion even more memorable she treated everyone to lemonade, cakes, chocolates and ice cream. Just as they were getting back into the coach to go home, she said to little Sally, 'Have you enjoyed yourself today?'

'Oh yes,' said Sally. 'It was lovely – except for the music, that is!'